INSTRUCTIONS FOR
AMERICAN SERVICEMEN IN
FRANCE
DURING WORLD WAR II

Pages 1–72 of this book are a facsimile of a "pocket guide" prepared by the Army Information Branch of the Army Service Forces, United States Army, in 1944.

INSTRUCTIONS FOR
AMERICAN SERVICEMEN IN
FRANCE
DURING WORLD WAR II

With a New Foreword by
Rick Atkinson

THE UNIVERSITY OF CHICAGO PRESS
CHICAGO AND LONDON

Pages 1–72 of this book are a facsimile of a "pocket guide" prepared by the Army Information Branch of the Army Service Forces, United States Army, in 1944.

This work is reproduced with the kind assistance of Mary Summerfield and of the Special Collections Research Center at Regenstein Library, the University of Chicago.

Rick Atkinson is the author of *An Army at Dawn: The War in North Africa, 1942–1943*, and *The Day of Battle: The War in Sicily and Italy, 1943–1944*, volumes one and two of *The Liberation Trilogy*, a narrative history of the American role in the European theater during World War II.

The University of Chicago Press, Chicago 60637
The University of Chicago Press, Ltd., London
Foreword © 2008 by Rick Atkinson
All rights reserved. Published 2008

Printed in the United States of America

17 16 15 14 13 12 11 10 09 08
1 2 3 4 5

ISBN-13: 978-0-226-84172-4 (cloth)
ISBN-10: 0-226-84172-3 (cloth)

Library of Congress
Cataloging-in-Publication Data

Pocket guide to France
Instructions to American servicemen in France during World War II / with a new foreword by Rick Atkinson.
    p. cm.
Originally published: A pocket guide to France / Army Information Branch of the Army Service Forces, United States Army. 1944.
ISBN-13: 978-0-226-84172-4 (cloth : alk. paper)
ISBN-10: 0-226-84172-3 (cloth : alk. paper)
1. France—Description and travel.
2. National characteristics, French.
3. World War, 1939–1945—France. I. United States. Army Service Forces. Information and Education Division. II. Title.
DC28.P63 2008
914.404'816—dc22

2007043865

⊗ The paper used in this publication meets the minimum requirements of the American National Standard for Information Sciences—Permanence of Paper for Printed Library Materials, ANSI Z-39.48-1992.

FOREWORD

Rick Atkinson

Amid the mountains of war materiel accumulating in southern England in the spring of 1944 were crates of a slender, highly classified book intended to give Allied soldiers a sense of the country they would soon overrun. One million copies of what was then titled *A Pocket Guide to France*, and has been retitled *Instructions for American Servicemen in France during World War II* for this edition, had been requested by the War Department in a top secret message, making the little volume among the most ambitious publishing ventures of World War II. As explained in a cable from Washington to the headquarters of General Dwight D. Eisenhower in London, the book was intended "to give a general idea of the country concerned, to serve as a guide to behavior in relation to the civil population, and to contain a suitable, concise vocabulary."

The "A.B.C. Booklets," as they were originally called, had a curious history. "What is being done in War Department to provide guides to countries of Europe?" a cable from London to Washington asked on December 17, 1943. "Many inquiries received." The reply came a day later, from Lieutenant General Brehon B. Somervell, the Army's chief logistician, to Lieutenant General John C. H. Lee, who served as Eisenhower's supply chief:

Short guides series now in preparation. . . . Includes manuscripts for Norway, Yugoslavia, France, Greece, Albania, Belgium, Netherlands, Denmark, Rumania, Hungary, Czechoslovakia, Bulgaria, Germany. Written by civilian and OSS [Office of Strategic Services, predecessor to the Central Intelligence Agency] experts, cleared by War Department agencies. Order of preparation determined priority. . . . Classified secret until distributed

The highest priority was assigned to the French guide, for it was on the beaches of Normandy that the Allied high command had agreed to launch Operation Overlord, the invasion of western Europe that would result in the final defeat of Nazi Germany. Initial printings would be made in England, to avoid security breaches in shipping so many books overseas, and then distributed to the troops aboard their invasion ships.

By mid-January 1944, Eisenhower's staff had begun to chafe at delays in receiving the manuscripts from which the guide would be printed. "When can arrival be expected of first copies?" a message to Washington asked on January 13. Another query followed a week later: "information requested when first finished manuscripts may be expected." The reply from the War Department on January 20 advised, "manuscripts of short guides to France, Holland, Norway, Belgium, Luxembourg . . . dispatched 17 January by courier pouch to chief of psychological warfare branch [in] your theater for clearance."

By early February, something clearly had gone awry. "Regarding guides to countries of Europe," Lee cabled Somervell on February 4. "What were article numbers given them by Army Courier Service in Foreign Mail Room Washington for pouch dispatched 17th Jan 44? . . . Copies of guides not received to date. Many inquiries regarding them."

The snafu came clear in Somervell's reply from Washington the following day. "These manuscripts were dispatched originally 15 January and were returned here unopened because erroneously addressed to Major General Robert H. McClure instead of correctly addressed to Brigadier General Robert A. McClure." The well-traveled documents were again dispatched, and placed in the hands of the proper McClure on February 9. Printing began soon after, and stacks of books joined the fifty thousand vehicles, four hundred and fifty thousand tons of ammunition, and countless sticks of chewing gum—to combat seasickness—accumulated for Overlord.

Like the vehicles and the ammo, the guide did its part to win the war. Soldiers were proselytized on the need to liberate France and the worthiness of the French to be liberated. Neither assertion was necessarily obvious to most GIs. France in 1940 had made a separate peace with the invading Germans, and the first enemies fought by American troops across the Atlantic were French soldiers and sailors in Morocco and Algeria during the North African invasion of November 1942. That was to be forgiven, if not quite forgotten, since many Frenchmen had since thrown in their lot with the Allied cause. "We are friends of the French and they are friends of ours," the guide instructs. "The Germans are our enemies and we are theirs."

If sometimes extraneous—did Private Smith really need to know that one hectoliter equals twenty-two gallons?—and occasionally patronizing of both GIs and Frenchmen—"Normandy looks rather like Ohio"—the guide evinces generosity, respect, and affection for suffering France. The liberators were told, accurately in this instance, to expect "a big welcome from the French. Americans are popular in France." Extracting France from German occupation had a flinty, practical purpose: "the enemy will be deprived of coal, steel, manpower, machinery, food, bases, seacoast and a long list of other essentials which have enabled him to carry on the war at the expense of the French."

Certainly the guide had its quirks, including a penchant for stereotype. The French were said to be "mentally quick," "economical," "realistic," and "individualists." They are "good talkers and magnificent cooks," but "they have little curiosity." Residents of Marseilles "are southern, turbulent and hot-headed." In an assertion that would seem especially suspect in a nation that championed the shrinking work week, the guide asserted, "respect for work is a profound principle in France."

Any GI inclined to bring home a French bride was advised that when the time came to ship out for home, "there will be no government transportation available for a wife." If facile, the advice tendered was sensible for any occupation army, then or now: "No bragging about anything. No belittling either. Be generous; it won't hurt. . . . Let us remember our likenesses, not our differences."

After four years of military occupation, and with two million Frenchmen held in Germany as war prisoners or slave laborers, "the French may not be able to be proud of how things look now so don't rub it in," the guide advises. In the event, the France discovered by the invading armies would indeed be despoiled, if not before the invasion then during and after. Some nine hundred thousand French buildings had been damaged or ruined in

World War I; that number would double in World War II, including two hundred thousand buildings demolished in Normandy alone.

The beginning of the end of France's subjugation began, famously, with eighteen thousand American and British paratroopers jumping into the Norman countryside before dawn on D-day. By midnight, more than one hundred and fifty thousand Allied troops were ashore, escorted by an armada that included six battleships, twenty-three cruisers, and eighty destroyers. The struggle for Normandy would prove to be "one terrible bloodletting," as the German Field Marshal Erwin Rommel observed, but by mid-August, GIs had reached the Loire at Nantes.

Eisenhower had intended to bypass Paris but changed his mind to exploit both the propaganda value of capturing the capital and to exploit the growing insurrection by Resistance fighters. On the morning of August 24, a French tank force entered the city from the south, greeted by delirious Parisians and German diehards at their barricades. Church bells pealed, snipers sniped, and at 2 p.m. on August 25 the German commander surrendered the city. In the ten weeks after D-day, at least fifty thousand Germans were killed, with two hundred thousand others captured and an estimated twelve hundred tanks lost.

One by one the cities fell: Lyon, Avignon, Boulogne. A Franco-American force of ninety-four thousand men landed on France's southern Mediterranean coast between Toulon and Cannes in Operation Dragoon; within a day they were twenty miles inland, and eventually extended the Allied front into Alsace.

Hitler ordered his occupation armies to retreat. The Allied drive would stall, temporarily stymied by stiffening German defenses, troublesome terrain, the obliteration of the French rail system, and shortages of fuel and ports. In December 1944, a final, futile German counteroffensive in the Belgian Ardennes and in Alsace led to the biggest battle on the western front, known as the Bulge. But by the end of 1944, the German thrust had spent itself; the end of the war in Europe was but five months away.

By January 1, 1945, 3.7 million Allied soldiers had come ashore in western Europe, disposed in three army groups, nine armies, twenty corps, and seventy-three divisions, two-thirds of them American. Allied casualties by this time totaled more than a half million, including 55,184 dead GIs.

France was free. As the little guide had predicted, "France will be liberated from the Nazi mob and the Allied armies will be that much nearer Victory."

Prepared by

ARMY INFORMATION BRANCH, A. S. F.

UNITED STATES ARMY

"You will probably get a rousing welcome from the French."

A POCKET GUIDE TO

France

WAR AND NAVY DEPARTMENTS, WASHINGTON, D. C.

CONTENTS

I

WHY YOU'RE GOING TO FRANCE

YOU are about to play a personal part in pushing the Germans out of France. Whatever part you take— rifleman, hospital orderly, mechanic, pilot, clerk, gunner, truck driver—you will be an essential factor in a great effort which will have two results: first, France will be liberated from the Nazi mob and the Allied armies will be that much nearer Victory, and second, the enemy will be deprived of coal, steel, manpower, machinery, food, bases, seacoast and a long list of other essentials which have enabled him to carry on the war at the expense of the French.

The Allied offensive you are taking part in is based upon a hard-boiled fact. It's this. We democracies aren't just doing favors in fighting for each other when history gets tough. We're all in the same boat. Take a look around you as you move into France and you'll see what the Nazis do to a democracy when they can get it down by itself.

In "Mein Kampf" Hitler stated that his plan was to destroy France first, then get England, after which he would have the United States cornered without a fight. The Allies are going to open up conquered France, re-establish the old Allied liberties and destroy the Nazi regime everywhere. Hitler asked for it.

You will probably get a big welcome from the French. Americans are popular in France. Your father or uncles who were in the A.E.F. may have told you about that. For the loyal French right now the arrival of American soldiers means freedom, food and a second chance to fight Hitler. That second chance is what French patriots have been waiting for.

Since June 1940 French men, women and even children have learned what happens to a great democracy when it collapses under the Nazi heel. For generations, France's motto on her public buildings has been Liberté, Egalité, Fraternité—Liberty, Equality, Fraternity. She lost all three when the Nazis marched in. Behind their Maginot Line the French thought it couldn't happen there. Against 42 million French citizens Hitler launched a totalitarian war machine composed of his 80 million subjects. In case you've heard Dr. Goebbels' story that

"The fall of Paris shook the world."

France was a pushover because she fell after six weeks' Blitzkrieg, just bear those figures in mind, plus the fact that in the last world war France held out for four years as the Allied battlefield. In 1918 French courage and endurance helped swing the Allied victory.

The causes of France's early collapse in this war were so complicated that even the French bitterly disagree as to who or what was to blame. It stands to reason you know less about it than they do. Our Sunday morning defeat at Pearl Harbor still galls us. France's defeat is a raw spot which the Nazis have been riding every day for nearly four years. Don't help them by making the French sore.

The main fact about France's defeat for you, an American soldier, is that when France fell, the biggest democracy in Europe went down, and with it, whether we all realized it or not, our last defense on the Continent against Hitler's crazy world conquest plan. As Europe's leading Republic, France was the keystone of freedom on land from the Mediterranean to the North Sea and one of the bulkheads of our freedom on the Atlantic. The fall of Paris shook the world.

II

THE UNITED STATES SOLDIER
IN FRANCE

Meet the People

MANY of you are no doubt wondering what kind of people the French are. You will soon see for yourselves. You will find that aside from the fact that they speak another (and very musical) language, they are very much like a lot of the people you knew back home. Here are a few facts about them which apply generally, but you must remember that each of them is an individual, and that Pierre Ducrot is as different from Paul Boucher as you are from Joe Jones.

Frenchmen are much like us in one particular respect—they are all Frenchmen together and are as intensely proud of the fact as we are of being Americans. Yet we have many kinds of Americans—Southerners, Yankees, Hoosiers, Native Sons—to name a few. The speech of your buddy from Brooklyn and the Mississippian's drawl wouldn't sound like the same language to most Frenchmen. It's the same with France; you will find many accents and dialects among Bretons, Alsatians, Normans, Basques, Catalans and Provençals—the Southerners of France. But these people are Frenchmen all, and proud of it.

You will soon discover for yourself that the French have what might be called a national character. It is made up of a half dozen outstanding characteristics:

(1) The French are mentally quick.

(2) Rich or poor, they are economical. Ever/ since the Nazis took over and French business came to a standstill, thousands of French families have kept themselves alive on their modest savings.

(3) The French are what they themselves call realistic. It's what we call having hard common sense. French common sense consists of looking the facts straight in the eye. Because they soon saw through the Nazi scheme of so-called collaboration, the Nazis have called the French cynical. Even in defeat the French can't be easily fooled.

(4) The French of all classes have respect for the traditionally important values in the life of civilized man. They have respect for religion and for artistic ideas. They have an extreme respect for property,

whether public or private. To them property represents the result of work. To destroy property means to belittle work. Respect for work is a profound principle in France. The Frenchman's woodpile is just as sacred to him as the *Banque de France*. Above all, the French respect the family circle as the natural center of social and economic life. France is not a country of eleven million homes. It is a country of eleven million family circles. There is very little divorce in France. The economies of French life are based on the parents' rule of working and saving for their children's future. French life is based on looking ahead.

(5) The French are individualists. The Frenchman believes in being yourself rather than the necessity of being like everybody else. This has its good as well as its bad side. It has often led the French into being a nation of biverse and even conflicting opinion. There aren't just two ways of looking at things in France—yours and the other fellow's. There are dozens of ways. Despite the political miseries this has recently brought to the French, France is still full of partisanships. Right now there are red hot topics which the French must decide for themselves. The future set-up in France is the Frenchman's business and nobody else's. His defeat has made him fear

for this future independence. The Allied invasion will bring up extra problems and lots of talk. Stay out of these local discussions, even if you have had French II in High School. In any French argument on internal French affairs, you will either be drowned out or find yourself involved in a first class French row. Quarrels between those who are fighting Hitler can still give him a big dangerous boost. He started this war on the principle of Divide and Conquer and his propaganda experts still believe they can make it work.

(6) The French are good talkers and magnificent cooks—if there still is anything left to put in the pot. French talk and French food have contributed more than anything else to the French reputation for gayety. Learn how to speak a few essential words of French. There is a glossary in the back of this book which will give you a brief vocabulary in French with pronunciations. Like most good talkers the French are polite. The courtesy words ("please"— "thank you" etc.) are the first things French children are taught.

The French also shake hands on greeting each other and on saying goodbye. They are not back-slappers. It's not their way.

In the larger cities you'll find shop-keepers who

speak English as do many small government func-
tionaries in big towns. Many of the younger French
generation have had a year in London or have picked
up a smattering of English, plus. slang, from the
American movies, which were their favorites till the
Nazis prohibited them.

You have certainly heard of gay Paree. Yet the
French have far less the regular habit of pleasure
than we Americans. Even before the Nazi occupation when the French were still free to have a good
time, they had it as a special event and managed it
thriftily. A whole French family would spend less on
pleasure in a month than you would over a week-end.
The French reputation for gayety was principally
built on the civilized French way of doing things; by
the French people's good taste; by their interest in
quality, not quantity; and by the lively energy of
their minds. The French are intelligent, have mostly
had a sensible education, without frills, are indus-
trious, shrewd and frugal.

The French are not given to confidences, or to tell-
ing how much money they make—or used to make—
or to bragging. And they think little of such talk
from others. The French have a remarkable capacity
for minding their own business. Even in the days
when they used to travel, before the Nazis shut down

"The French have a remarkable capacity
for minding their own business."

on it, the French never used to sit down in a railway train and tell their private affairs to a total stranger. They are observant; don't think they won't notice what you do. But they have little curiosity.

Security and Health

You probably won't get mixed up with anything as glamorous as Mata Hari—the Germans have wised up and are sending around much less obvious spies these days. Don't forget that along with the Nazi army of occupation came the Gestapo almost four years ago. You can be sure that by this time their system for finding out what Hitler and his bullies want to know is working pretty smoothly. The best thing for you to do is to keep any information of value to the enemy which may have come your way strictly to yourself. The Frenchmen with whom you make friends won't be offended if you become silent as a stone when military subjects come up. Far from it. They will applaud you, since they have had to learn the value of silence themselves during the occupation. Be as friendly as you like with anyone who wants to share your friendship; just don't discuss anything connected with the operations of your unit or of any other you may have heard about. Remember the wolf in sheep's clothing.

Many of the so-called French prostitutes right now have been drawn from the dregs of other occupied countries and are deliberately planted under-cover Nazi agents. You are particularly interesting to them, for they might pick up something about your job as an American soldier which would be useful and valuable to the Nazi secret service. You and your outfit might later pay with your lives as a result of your having talked and the Nazi agents' having been able to put two and two together. Or you might catch a disease and thus make one less good healthy soldier in our fighting force. Make no mistake about this. Nazi propagandists have planned it both ways.

Almost anybody in France can get chummy with a special sort of hard-boiled dame who, for obvious business reasons, is sitting alone at a café table. It's so easy that many of the better cafés will not permit women who come in alone even to sit down. Cafés which specialize in a prostitute clientele are usually clip joints. This goes double for the night dancing places where tarts congregate.

While it is true that the French point of view toward sex is somewhat different from the American, it does not follow that illicit sex relations are any safer than in the United States. As a matter of fact there is a greater risk of contracting venereal diseases.

Before the war the French Government made an attempt to examine and license prostitutes. But don't be fooled. No system of examination has ever made a prostitute safe. Her health card means absolutely nothing.

If a girl doesn't carry a prostitute's card, then she is an "irregular." She may be picked up by the police for illegal soliciting and involve you in unpleasantness. But "regular" or "irregular" either kind can present you with a nasty souvenir of Paris to take back home. Don't take chances with your health and your future. If you have been exposed to infection never fail to report at once for prophylactic treatment.

Health conditions of France closely resemble those you know in the United States except for a somewhat lower sanitary standard. Water supplies in the rural areas are more likely to be polluted but those of the large cities were generally safe before the war. Milk is not safe to drink unless boiled. Don't experiment too much with "French cooking" unless you pick a good place.

Flies, lice and fleas are more common than with us, and less is done about them. Although they used to spread very little disease in times of peace, conditions are such today that they may be far more dangerous. For your own sake keep them away.

You Are a Guest of France.

If you are billeted with a French family, you will be in a more personal relation than if you were in barracks or a hotel. Remember that the man of the house may be a prisoner of the Nazis, along with a million and one half others like him. Treat the women in the house the way you want the women of your family treated by other men while you're away.

The household you are billeted with will probably want to show how they feel toward America and Americans. This will entail responsibilities you'll have to live up to. Mostly, the French think Americans always act square, always give the little fellow a helping hand and are good-natured, big-hearted and kind. They look up to the United States as the friend of the oppressed and the liberator of the enslaved. The French trust both you and your country more than they do most other men and nations.

If the French at home or in public try to show you any hospitality, big or little—a home cooked meal or a glass of wine—it means a lot to them. Be sure you thank them and show your appreciation. If madame invites you to a meal with the family, go slow. She'll do her best to make it delicious. But what is on the table may be all they have and what they must use as left-overs for tomorrow or the rest of the week.

And give her a hand around the house to help with the extra work you make by being there. French women are still talking about how your fathers helped out occasionally in the A.E.F. The French mother of a family has been carrying on without a husband to help with wages or the heavy work. She hasn't had enough soap to keep things clean or thread and needles to keep clothes mended. When there hasn't been enough food to go 'round among the children, the mothers have deprived themselves.

Mademoiselle

France has been represented too often in fiction as a frivolous nation where sly winks and coy pats on the rear are the accepted form of address. You'd better get rid of such notions right now if you are going to keep out of trouble. A great many young French girls never go out without a chaperone, day or night. It will certainly bring trouble if you base your conduct on any false assumptions.

France is full of decent women and strict women. Most French girls have less freedom than girls back home. If you get a date, don't be surprised if her parents want to meet you first, to size you up. French girls have been saying "No" to the Nazi soldiers and officers for years now. They expect the men in the American Army to act like friends and Allies.

Should you find some girl whose charms induce thoughts of marriage, here are a few points to think over: In your present status as a soldier, marriage to a foreign girl has many complications. The same reasons that caused so many of your comrades, and possibly yourself, to forego marriage at home—the uncertainty of future movements, the hazards a soldier faces—apply here even more so. From time to time, regulations may vary with regard to marriage abroad, but here are some ideas as to what you may run into:

During the war and for six months thereafter the government will not pay for the transportation of dependents of military personnel from a theater of operations to the U. S. nor from theater to theater.

After the war, when you are shipped home for discharge, there will be no government transportation available for a wife. Nor is there likely to be any for a long, long time.

In any case you can't marry without the permission of your commanding officer.

★————————★

III

A FEW PAGES OF FRENCH HISTORY

Occupation

Continental France has been directly occupied in part since 1940, and totally since November 1942. The Germans have stripped her bare. The Germans who occupied France were not only soldiers. They brought in engineers, bankers, business men, and specialists of every kind for the purpose not merely of administering but of depleting the territory. They levied a war indemnity purported to cover only costs of operation but which yielded huge sums over and above those costs. The Germans made an inventory of the possessions of the nation. Bit by bit they moved to Germany everything not required by them in France to carry on their war Only those things needed for military purposes and for the welfare of their troops and agents in France were left behind. They starved the French people both by requisitioning the food supply and by creating black markets in which they bought up most of what was left.

Almost all French civilians are grievously under-nourished, and many have starved to death. The Nazis have eaten the food, drunk the wine, and shipped almost everything else back to Germany.

You have no doubt known wartime shortages of things you are used to having, but you can have no idea of what it means to be faced with a hopeless scarcity of the commonest articles. Ration coupons are issued for everything, but often they prove to be useless little scraps of paper. To get a few withered vegetables, housewives stand in line for hours on end in the cold—only to turn away empty handed because the trucks have been intercepted on their way to market. Bread, poor as it is, is always hard to come by. Little morsels of what the conquerors are pleased to call soap are doled out every now and then. When there are any at all, three cigarettes a day are all anyone ever gets. The towns have suffered most, but life in the country has been no picnic.

A great French tradition has been justifiable pride in a long and illustrious military history. A large part of the sense of humiliating tragedy which swept over France when she fell in 1940 derived from the spectacle of the apparent ruin of her military honor. The German conquest was so overwhelmingly sudden and complete after the demoralizing cynicism

"*To get a few withered vegetables, housewives stand in line for hours only to turn away empty handed because the trucks have been intercepted on their way to market.*"

★━━━★

of the "Phony War" (September 1939–May 1940) that the Allied armies were caught with their pants down. The struggle soon proved hopeless, and with her head bowed, France capitulated.

Though both Britain and France suffered great losses in the defeat, the British were able to save the bulk of their Army in the heroic escape at Dunkirk. Some citizens of France in defeat have harbored bitter feelings toward their British allies. Don't you help anybody to dig up past history in arguments. This is a war to fight the Nazis, not a debating society.

The French underground—composed of millions of French workers, patriots, college professors, printers, women, school children, people in all walks of life of the real true-hearted French—has worked courageously at sabotage of Nazi occupation plans. Nazi censorship and Nazi firing squads have tried to prevent your hearing about this resistance. Dr. Goebbels tried to stuff the world's ears with the story of French collaboration with Germany. The only good collaboration today is the collaboration of the old democratic Allies.

Remember the Frenchmen who were able to escape from France and rally to the Tricolor, and the fighting record they made for themselves in the

Tunisian Campaign and in Italy. The heroic struggle put up by the Fighting French at Bir Hakeim, in the Lybian Campaign, will live long in the annals of military enterprise.

There are some 1¼ million French prisoners of war held in Germany. A million others have been taken as workers to the war factories of Germany, and another 150,000 have been behind bars and barbed wire in their own country. For such activities as derailing German troop trains and helping Allied soldiers and fliers out of the country, one Frenchman was shot every two hours, on the average, year in and year out. And though Hitler's propaganda experts still shout that France pulled out of this present war and left you to help do the fighting for them, the facts prove the contrary. In the six week Battle of France, from May 10 to June 22, 1940, 108,000 were killed, 260,000 were wounded.

Resistance.

The details of fliers' escapes, after having had to bail out over France, are never made public, for obvious reasons. But time after time, our fliers have come back to base after having fallen into the very jaws of the Nazis. For every one of our returned fliers, several French lives have been risked. In spite of the eternal anti-Allied propaganda by means of which the Goebbels-controlled press and radio of France have tried to convince the French that they have been betrayed by the greedy, self-seeking Allied powers, the French remain our Allies. There had grown up in France a movement of resistance to the occupying forces and of aid to the Allies which has constituted in effect a continuation of the war by the French people despite the armistice of 1940. And this resistance has been carried out in the face of an enemy who desperately needed, for military purposes, the cooperation which he never got from any but a handful of profiteers and fascists among the French people. Although deprived of the means of making war in its steel and gunpowder aspects, the French have kept up the fight in France by sabotage, by the publication of underground newspapers and by other means, all involving grave risks for the patriots.

Necessary Surgery

Some French families have been made homeless or have lost relatives or both as a direct result of Allied bombings. Most of them have understood the tragic necessity for this. Some, as a result of stray bombs, have not. But most of them agree that the tentacles of the Nazi octopus must be sought out and destroyed wherever they have entwined themselves. That German war installations were discovered in France in areas thickly populated by Frenchmen and their families, whom we had no wish to harm, has been a constant source of concern to the directors of Allied operations. But the plants and installations had to go, whatever the cost.

A Quick Look Back

As a country France is a small place to have pulled such a big weight as she has over the centuries. You could put nearly all of France into our two states of Utah and Nevada.

But the history of France goes back for two thousand years. If you studied Latin at High School and had to wade through Julius Caesar, you may remember that he opens up by saying, "All Gaul is divided into three parts." The Gaul he was referring to was France. Even in Caesar's time there was a settlement on the River Seine which became the Paris of today.

For the last nine hundred years France has ranked as one of the world's great civilizations. Her books, writers, artists, universities and industries, like her silk weaving, and her prosperous towns, were famous. The French were noted for their taste in fashions when Christopher Columbus was setting out to discover America. Shortly after our Pilgrim Fathers landed on their barren Plymouth Rock in 1620, Louis XIV, the most celebrated French monarch, began his long, record-breaking reign of 72 years. The magnificence of his Court dazzled the world and he built France into the most powerful State in Europe. Under his sway, French became the language of international diplomacy and still is.

The growth of democratic ideas sprang up at the same time both in France and in the American colonies, and a few years after our own American Revolutionary War, the ideal of freedom for the common man was proclaimed in Europe by the French Revolution. Out of that struggle came Napoleon, whom the French revere as a great military leader, and founder of the Code Napoléon, which is still in effect. Napoleon rose and fell, but the France of ideas lived on.

Not only French ideas but French guns helped us to become a nation. Don't forget that liberty loving Lafayette and his friends risked their lives and fortunes to come to the aid of General George Washington at a moment in our opening history when nearly all the world was against us. In the War for Independence which our ragged army was fighting, every man and each bullet counted. Frenchmen gave us their arms and their blood when they counted most. Some 45,000 Frenchmen crossed the Atlantic to help us. They came in cramped little ships of two or three hundred tons requiring two months or more for the crossing. We had no military engineers; French engineers designed and built our fortifications. We had little money; the French lent us over six million dollars and gave us over three million more.

In the same fighting spirit we acted as France's ally in 1917 and 1918 when our A.E.F. went into action. In that war, France, which is about a fourteenth of our size, lost nearly eighteen times more men than we did, fought twice as long and had an eighth of her country devastated.

Churchgoers

Throughout the history of France, the Church has filled a very real compartment in the lives of Frenchmen. In the Middle Ages and during the Renaissance, the superb craftsmanship and the sincere religious feeling of the French combined to erect some of the most magnificent monuments to God ever created. You will no doubt see some of the great cathedrals of France. Moderated by a spirit of tolerance learned in the bloody religious wars and persecutions of the past, the same spirit that built these matchless cathedrals exists in France today. The vast majority of the French are Catholics. There are about a million Protestants in the country. Churches, from the great cathedrals down to the smallest parish chapels, are crowded on Sundays and Saints' Days. The Parish priest, "Monsier le curé", has great influence in the community, and lives among his flock as one of them, taking an active interest in their comings and goings, and especially in the education of the young. It is easy to imagine how the French feel about the pagan ideologies of the Nazis. The feeling gives them yet another incentive towards the banishment of Hitler's "New Order."

The Machinery

It is just as well that you know something about the French system of conducting public business. Before the war, the Third Republic (1870–1940) had as its chief executive a president, as we do. The presidential term of office in France was seven years. The legislative body consisted of a Senate and a

"Monsieur le Maire."

Chamber of Deputies, on the whole very similar to our Congress. One striking difference between the French political system and our own was that where we have several political parties, the very large majority of voters being included in only two of them, the French had a great many parties running the whole range of political thought from extreme radicalism to reactionary conservatism. This diversified party system made for frequent cabinet shake-ups, many cabinets lasting for a relatively short time. Any group retaining control for over a year was an exception. This sytem was an expression of the intense individualism of the French.

Let's look at the local subdivisions of this national system. France is divided into 90 counties. For our "county" the French say "Département". The Départements subdivide themselves into Arrondissements, each containing Cantons, which are made up of groups of Communes. The men of each Commune (women have never voted in France) elect a Mayor (*Maire*), who is the local official with whom your unit is likely to have the most contact. He will no doubt have much to do with the billeting arrangements, water supply, traffic control, and other such administrative details. Remember that he is quite an important figure in the community. He will rate any courtesies paid him, and will no doubt be of great help to your unit.

IV

OBSERVATION POST

The Provinces

While you are in France you are most likely to
be located in the provinces, so you had better have
some idea of what they are like. Paris can come later.

The 35 million French who do not live in Paris will
be quick to tell you that Paris is not France. We
have the same idea at home when we say New York
isn't the United States.

The French provinces are all of France—except
Paris and the Ile de France district immediately
surrounding it. So the French provinces and the people in them are the major and most representative
part of the country. The French provincials are the
people who really keep the country going. They are
the ordinary, average people. They make France.
They are France.

French provincial towns, especially if they are of
the picturesque variety, might have more charm and
beauty than some of our small towns, but not neces-

sarily as much entertainment. French provincial towns are about like what your home town was when your father was a boy, before movies, the radio and the family car changed all that. Your father wasn't bored. Neither are the provincial French. The provinces are a good place for you to learn what the French really are and to show them what real Americans are like.

For the past years the BBC (London) and, since February 1942, OWI's "Voice of America" have been the chief sources of true world news for the French. During the most trying years, the BBC, and later our own programs have been sources of consolation and hope for delivery from Nazi tyranny. The French never listened to the enemy radio, and with the return of Laval in April 1942 they ceased to pay any attention to the German controlled traitors' radio of Vichy and Paris.

The Cafes

Public entertainment in any French town centers in its cafés. To the French the café is much more and much less than a bar. It's the social center. There a man takes his family of an afternoon or after the evening meal to have a coffee, a glass of beer or wine,

"French provincial town."

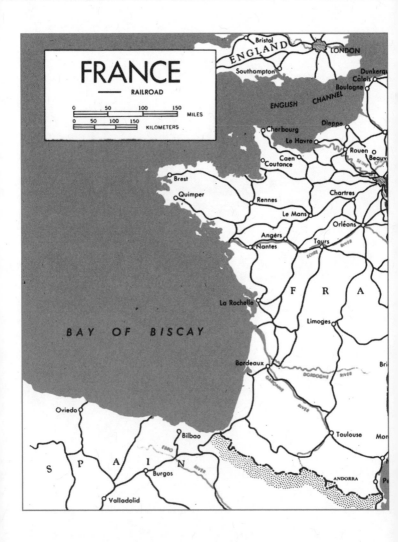

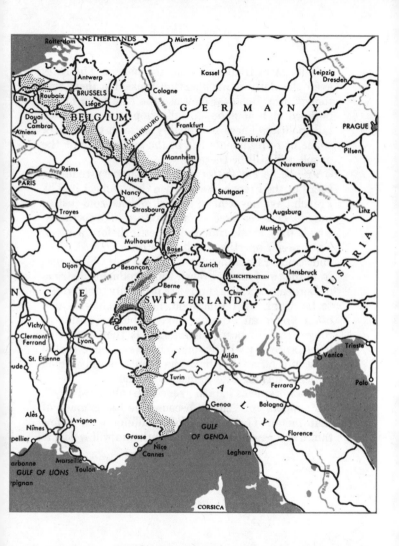

to talk, meet friends or read the papers. The cafés keep the daily newspapers on racks for their customers' use. Business men use the café for a neighborhood club at noon, to talk shop, close a deal or talk politics. There is probably little in the way of coffee or refreshments left in the cafés now but the people will still be there.

French beer is flatter and more slippery than our beer but the French like it, when they can get it. The French have never liked their drinks ice-cold just as they have never liked strong mixtures like cocktails, which they think ruin the appetite before a meal. They prefer apertifs which are mostly cooked wines and stronger than they look. The red and white wines from the two famous French wine-producing districts of Bordeaux and Burgundy are primarily table wines, to be drunk with your food, but French workmen often prefer an evening glass of blanc (white) or rouge (red) to beer. Champagne is that expensive fizzy processed white wine. The Nazis have carted most of it off as they have the French brandy which Hitler is turning into industrial alcohol.

The workmen's bars in France are called "bistros", "estaminets" or "zincs" because the bar is made of that metal. These are humble affairs with a few tables and sawdust floor. The workman will welcome you; he is a regular fellow. In his velveteen pantaloons and beret he will look more picturesque than his opposite number back home in the United States. He is what the French call *le peuple*—The People. They have more sense, resistance and pride than any other class in France.

Important: Don't forget that in the French café or restaurant you always tip the waiter 10 percent of the bill when he brings it to your table. This 10 percent is a regular thing. The French give it and so must you. It's not just so much velvet for the waiter; it is what he mostly has to live on. If you as a foreigner have asked for special considerations or help in any restaurant or café, it would be fair if you gave a few francs extra on your tip. Don't change your money into francs at bars or in shops. The rate will not be so good.

In the workmen's bars and cafés the Frenchmen play belotte, a two-handed card game something like pinochle. In the cafés there are or used to be dominoes, chess and backgammon boards for the customers. There is little canned entertainment in French cafés.

The neighborhood French café is the most French thing in all France. If you want to be welcome when you come back a second time use the café the way

---

the French do. As you'll see by looking around you, the Frenchman comes there with his family. It is NOT a place where the French go to get drunk. Like all wine-drinking people, the French don't drink to get drunk. Drunkeness is rare in France.

Conversely, the only thing the French have never been able to say against the Nazi Army of Occupation is that it was a drunken army. Don't let them say it about the American Army. And don't forget that the Nazi propaganda agents have already given the French a pretty picture of the way some Americans act on Saturday night.

Respect Frenchmen's belongings. If you were a cut-up back home, remember you are not at home now. The quickest way to get the local French angry with your outfit is for some members to rough-house and destroy any French property.

The Farms

With two million Frenchmen still prisoners in Germany, either in concentration camps or as factory labor slaves, you probably won't find the French towns, houses, roads or farms in good condition. Thousands of American tourists a year used to flock to France because its beauties and picturesque landscape made it a show place. The French may not be able to be proud of how things look now so don't rub it in. Just remember that a sixth of their civilian population was dꞏiven down the roads when the Nazis invaded northern France. Lots of these people lost every stick of furniture they possessed and doubled up far from home with other families in discomfort and poverty. French factories were taken over by Hitler's agents. The French have had nothing new to wear for over three years. Farmers have had to make bread out of the seed they were saving for the spring planting.

Under these typical Nazi conditions no French farm can look its best though French farmers are among the best there are. They form the largest single class in France. About 40 percent of France's population ordinarily lives on the soil and constitutes what is called the peasant class. Don't think that peasant means hick in French. The French peasants are shrewd, hard-headed, successful and conservative.

For instance you'd be making a mistake to suppose that just because the French peasant still ploughs with horses, if there are any left, or even oxen, that he's not smart. He knows what he's doing and why. The French farmer has always used and bred a specially large, handsome farm horse called the Percheron.

The peasant's wooden shoes are part of his thrift. France has no hot summer days and nights like ours in the Middle West. And the land is not deforested because the French have for centuries re-planted the trees they cut. Thus French rivers run deep the year 'round and the French soil is cool and moist. The peasant wears wooden shoes because they insulate his feet against the damp and mud better than leather. He may look picturesque. His aim is to be practical. His friendliness can be important to you.

For generations, from father to son, the French peasant made a good living and salted away a little cash. Lots of families have been farming the same ground for over a thousand years. Pep talks about labor saving devices or electrical gadgets are also not likely to interest the French farmer. He knows his own business and has prospered on it in peace. He uses candles or coal-oil lamps like your grandparents. His wife makes her hearth broom from twigs cut from the hedge-row. The French peasant's farming theory is simple—to use everything, to waste nothing. His small farm pays. A hundred acres is a big farm in France. Land is precious. To own your own land is to be somebody. Small as France is, it has about the same variety of crops we have back home.

The Regions

The richest farms in France are in Normandy, the butter, egg, cheese and grazing country. You've probably sung "When It's Apple Blossom Time in Normandy." The apple orchards there are a big produce market item. Rouen is the largest inland Norman port on the River Seine. Normandy looks rather like Ohio. Brittany, a projecting arm of land across from the south of England, is poorer land, but raises a big potato crop. Most of the sailors in the French Navy which sank its fleet at Toulon harbor are Brittany boys. The Bretons, as they call themselves, are fisher folk. They sail their schooners once a year to the Newfoundland Banks for cod. Many of the canned sardines you used to eat at home came from Brittany waters. The wheat district or bread basket of France is south west of Paris on the plains of the Beauce, near the grain center and cathedral market town of Chartres. There is a small mountainous center ridge across the lower middle of France, called the Central Massive range where sheep are raised and wool is carded and woven. Just north of this range are many health centers, established around thermal springs, like our White Sulphur Springs. The town of Vichy, seat of the French government under Marshal Pétain, is a thermal spring town.

"Don't think that peasant
means hick in France."

The French Riviera is the coastal strip which extends from the Italian border on the east back toward Marseilles. The Riviera landscape and climate is like California. But the expensive California irrigations systems which have reclaimed its dry land have never been installed on the Riviera. Its main crop has always been jasmine flowers and roses, raised for France's perfume manufacturing center in the hill town of Grasse. For the rest, the farmers, many of mixed Italian blood, grow olive trees, for oil, raise green stuffs like peas or artichokes but can grow no potatoes, cattle or heavy grain. Thus the people on the Riviera suffered more from hunger than other districts, when transportation broke down. Whereas adults all over France lost an average of forty pounds each from malnutrition under the Nazis, the Riviera children developed rickets from hunger. Few babies were born alive in this district, owing to the dire food conditions. Live strictly on your rations in the Riviera, or you may deprive others whose need is greater than yours.

The main cities of the Riviera are Nice, a handsome old resort city, and Cannes, which is modern. It was the chief summer resort and beach life center of France and was developed mostly since the last war. Both cities are elegant, with big hotels, sea promenades and avenues of palms and, like the many small fishing ports along the coast, worth visiting on your leave. Behind the coast lie the lower stretches of the French Alps. Near the Swiss border there are skiing resorts.

Just west of the Riviera district proper lies Marseilles, the oldest and biggest colonial port of France. The French Empire in North Africa is relatively new and has been developed only in the last fifty years, and Marseilles is the port of entry for supplies from the colonies. Though Marseilles, like the southern two fifths of France, was technically supposed to be Unoccupied France, the Nazi armistice commission agents managed to control all the food landed at the port, always the food depot of the south. The population of the city, forced to unload and transport food it was never allowed to eat, staged many food riots. When the Nazis occupied all of France, at the time of the Anglo-American liberation of North Africa, November 7, 1942, the Nazis were already taking 60 percent of the food that passed into Marseilles. Like many port towns Marseilles can be tough. Its people are southern, turbulent and hot-headed. The French national anthem, the Marseillaise, was a Revolutionary hymn that honored the city's love for liberty.

We have saved to the last the region of France which for two reasons the Nazis were most interested in. This is the Channel section, from Dunkirk on down along the coast. It is the section directly across from England. It is the section from which the Nazis hoped to invade England. It is also the heavy industries region of France, the second reason for the Nazi interest in it. Here are the coal mines which run over the border into Belgium, the steel centers, the cotton spinning mills at Roubaiz and Cambrai. To bolster their own production, the Nazis declared this whole Channel section a Forbidden Zone. French from other districts were not allowed to enter. The French living there were forced into labor gangs on the Nazi production line. Letters were not allowed to come in or go out. Dunkirk, and Dieppe, before the war were ports for Channel steamers plying between England and France. Le Havre, at the mouth of the River Seine, was the port for the French transatlantic ships sailing out to New York.

The Workers

The skilled French workmen, like those in the Forbidden Zone and in the automobile industry located in the outskirts of Paris, have suffered great humiliation under the Nazis. French labor unions were well organized. Many of their leaders have been shot by the Nazis. French commerce has been completely crippled by the Nazi occupation because France was a land not of big department stores and interlocking organizations, but of little shops, operated by the owner and often his wife. Such little shops were easily driven to the wall by Nazi tactics.

You'll notice in what is left of French commerce that the French woman plays a big part. Madame usually sits behind the cash box in the shop, Monsieur, her husband, does the selling. He is legally head of the business and of the family but she personally manages the accounts and the cash and is the head of the home. The authority is divided, each one shoulders his and her share. French women have had a lot to do with France's thrift and prosperity in the past and have helped keep the country going while their husbands were prisoners in Germany. On the farms the women have plowed and planted, girls and grandmothers have reaped and gleaned the harvest. They haven't worn any uniforms but they have served their country well. In the cities they have run the shops alone as long as there was goods to sell. They have fed their children horse meat when other food failed. They educated them at home when

the schools broke down. French women deserve the
right sort of appreciation.

The Tourist

In case you get leave, and want to enjoy being a
tourist for a change, here are a few notes.

There are few French towns that haven't something worth seeing. The French countryside is dotted
with châteaux. These were the country mansions of
the noble families in the old days. Some of them are
regular castles with moat, drawbridge and formal
gardens. They are often·open to the public on certain days, for a small visitors' fee.

Many provincial cities have important museums
(buy a ticket) with a display of beautiful things
French workers have made, maybe hundreds of years
ago. Until the Nazis stole anything they wanted,
most of the museums had ancient tapestries and a
picture gallery. In the United States our galleries
and museums are filled with art imported at great
price from Europe.

The churches are usually ancient and the best
architecture the towns or villages possess. The
French are proud of their church architecture. Don't
forget they are largely a Catholic people. They will

be glad to have you visit their churches like thousands of American tourists before you but they will
naturally expect you to treat them as places of wor-
ship, not as stations of a noisy sight-seeing tour.
Don't try to visit churches during service.

Many of the largest churches such as those in the
ancient Normandy towns of Coutance, Caen, Beau-
vais, or the walled abbey of Mont St. Michel were
built around the year 1200. They are Gothic in style,
with elaborate stone carvings, traceries, the oldest
stained glass windows still standing, and pointed
arch construction.

The past is still close to every Frenchman's life
because his family and ancestors made it.

But don't get the idea that the French can't build
something up-to-date when they choose. In Paris
they built the Eiffel Tower long before we had our
Empire State skyscraper in New York. For years the
Eiffel Tower was the tallest construction man had
ever erected and still comes close to it.

If you get to Paris, the first thing to do is to buy
a guide book, if there are any left after the Nazi
tourists' departure. Paris is in a sense the capital of
Europe and regarded as one of the most beautiful
and interesting cities in the world. We don't know
just what the war has done to Paris. These notes will

assume that there'll still be lots to see.

Decide what you want to see. Consult your guidebook's map of the city. The Paris buses are plainly marked by letters or numbers which correspond to guide book indications. Be your own guide. So-called professional Paris guides might be crooks.

Bus stops, every few blocks, are marked by signs on lamp posts, bearing the letter or number of the bus which passes there. First class up front, second class in back. The Metro or subway also has two classes. There are large maps of the city with the Metro routes and station names plainly marked, in each Metro station. A map of the routes, with indications where to transfer under ground, is posted in each subway coach.

To get an idea where you are and what Paris is like, start with a walk on the boulevards around the Place de l'Opéra. To begin with, the interior of the Opéra is well worth a look: traditional red silk, gilded carving and plush. You will probably want to see Napoleon's tomb in the Invalides where the French Army Staff had its offices. The cathedral of Notre Dame is the most famous church in Paris. You've surely seen it in the movies and will probably want to see the real thing. It is on the River Seine which winds through Paris, with poplar trees growing on either side, in the cobblestone landing quais below the street level. You can walk from Notre Dame to the Louvre, along the river, in half an hour. The Louvre is France's greatest art gallery and used to be the palace of the kings. The Venus di Milo and the Mona Lisa have been the Louvre's most famous single pieces of sculpture and portraiture, but the war may have caused their removal—whether by the French for safekeeping, or by the Nazis for their art lover, Field Marshal Goering, we would not know at the moment. A new series of modern buildings and an esplanade were built as approaches to the Eiffel Tower shortly before the war began. The Place de la Concorde, with fountains and an obelisk Napoleon brought back from his conquest of Egypt, is at the foot of the Champs-Elysées. This avenue slopes up to the Arc de Triomphe and the Tomb of the Unknown Soldier. Behind the Arc de Triomphe the Avenue Foch, named for the World War French generalissimo, leads to the Bois de Bologne, Paris' largest forest and park. Up on the hill, overlooking Paris, is Montmartre.

French railroad equipment will probably shock you. It shocks the French. The Nazis took their best rolling stock. Before the war the French had some of the fastest short distance trains in the world.

There are three classes of French passenger cars, first, second and third. First class ranks with our extra fare trains; second ranks with our parlor car and third class is like our ordinary day coach. If third class French coaches sometimes have wooden instead of upholstered seats, and are less comfortable than our day coach, remember that they are also less expensive. It all evens up.

Important: You must buy your railway ticket and show it to the ticket-taker at the gate which leads to the train platforms before you get on a French train. More important: Don't throw away your ticket on the train. It has to be punched again on the train and taken up by a ticket taker in the station at the end of your journey. He is part of the French system of checking to see that all passengers have bought tickets. If you can't give him your ticket at your journey's end, you might have to buy another.

French hotel bills are complicated. To avoid discussion afterward, make sure you know the price of your room before you take it. If the landlord speaks no English and you no French, ask him "Combien" (see glossary) and indicate that you want him to write down the price so you can be sure there is no misunderstanding. Try to compare prices in a couple of establishments before making your choice or

"Paris street scene."

"Rue Francois Miron."

starting an endless argument.

When you get your hotel bill, there will be added to it a straight 10 percent (or 12 percent in bigger places) for Service. This automatic payment, in lieu of a voluntary tip to the personnel who have served you, is the French law. It is the way that the French hotel keepers and the French hotel unions decided, a few years before the war, was the fairest arrangement for both sides. Except in swank hotels, this service tax lets you out of having to tip down the line of chambermaids, waiters, etc., on leaving. There might also be, in certain districts, a very slight fractional "taxe de ségour" or residence tax on your hotel bill. If so it's also the law. If your small hotel has a bathtub still operating and coal for hot water, ask to have a bath drawn for you. It will cost a few francs extra. Rooms with private bath are still de luxe in France. Meals served in your room will have a small extra service charge.

Remember that if you eat your meals in the diningroom and do NOT have them charged on your bill, but pay them on the spot, the waiter is still entitled to his personal 10 percent when he brings you his bill for the meal. If you didn't tip him then, he'd get nothing. Figure it out. If there is no hotel diningroom, often the case in little inns, your break-

---

fast will be brought to your bedroom without extra charge. (That would be one of the services your 10 percent service tax would be paying for.) The French never went in for a breakfast of eggs, toast, orange, juice, etc. They still take coffee with milk and bread and butter—if they can find it.

When you ride in a taxi, tip 10 percent of the fare. A franc (maybe more now) is charged for each piece of luggage. This is the law. Porters at railway stations also charge (or did) one franc for each valise they carry. You also tip ushers at movies and theaters for finding your seat.

It used to be a half franc at the movies and a franc at the theater. All these little tips in France or the hotel service tax merely mean that the customer pays directly for service given him and not for service given someone else, as figured in our more costly American overhead. People who work on the tip system in France are given an insignificant wage and the tips are the rest of their salary. Tips are not just gouging. They are part of a low cost system.

Don't expect French plumbing in hotels, railway stations or homes to be like modern American plumbing. It isn't. The French would appreciate an up-to-date American bathroom, with all the gadgets, but have never been able to afford it. After all, maybe your grandad wasn't brought up in one either and he manged to survive. Few homes or apartments outside of Paris have steam heat though most hotels do. Now they may not have the coal.

V

IN PARTING

We are friends of the French and they are friends of ours.

The Germans are our enemies and we are theirs. Some of the secret agents who have been spying on the French will no doubt remain to spy on you. Keep a close mouth. No bragging about anything.

No belittling either. Be generous; it won't hurt.

Eat what is given you in your own unit. Don't go foraging among the French. They can't afford it.

Boil all drinking water unless it has been approved by a Medical Officer.

You are a member of the best dressed, best fed, best equipped liberating Army now on earth. You are going in among the people of a former Ally of your country. They are still your kind of people who happen to speak democracy in a different language. Americans among Frenchmen, let us remember our likenesses, not our differences. The Nazi slogan for destroying us both was "Divide and Conquer." Our American answer is "In Union There Is Strength."

Gendarme

ANNEX:

VARIOUS AIDS

DECIMAL SYSTEM

In France, almost all calculations are based on the decimal system. We are here concerned with weights and measures, and money. As we have dollars and cents, the French have centimes and francs. 100 cents to the dollar; 100 centimes to the franc. The value of the franc has never been as much as the value of the dollar. You will be told how many cents a franc is worth before you have occasion to use one. There is just one small complication in the French monetary system—the sou (say "soo"). A sou is five centimes—twenty sous to the franc. Don't throw your money away. You'll only force prices up; and they're high enough as it is. Send your extras home.

Weights and measures in France conform to the metric system, which is in use throughout most of Europe. This is also a decimal system: larger units are divisible by ten or a hundred to give smaller units. The following table of approximate comparisons may prove useful:

$$
\begin{aligned}
10 \text{ centimeters} &= 4 \text{ inches} \\
11 \text{ meters} &= 12 \text{ yards} \\
8 \text{ kilometers} &= 5 \text{ miles} \\
50 \text{ kilometers} &= 31 \text{ miles} \\
26 \text{ sq. kilometers} &= 10 \text{ square miles} \\
1 \text{ hectare} &= 2\tfrac{1}{2} \text{ acres} \\
15 \text{ grams} &= \tfrac{1}{2} \text{ ounce} \\
5 \text{ kilos} &= 11 \text{ pounds} \\
1 \text{ hectoliter} &= 22 \text{ gallons} \\
1 \text{ metric ton} &= 2{,}205 \text{ pounds}
\end{aligned}
$$

$$
\text{One meter} = \left\{ \begin{array}{l} 1{,}000 \; \textit{milli}\text{meters} \\ 100 \; \textit{centi}\text{meters} \\ 10 \; \textit{deci}\text{meters} \end{array} \right\} = 3' \; 3\tfrac{3}{8}''
$$

1,000 meters = 1 kilometer = ⅝ mile
1 kilogram (kilo) = 2.2 pounds
1 liter = ⅘ quart

You will soon get used to dealing in terms of these measures, just as you will quickly gain familiarity with the coins and paper you will use for money.

FRENCH LANGUAGE GUIDE

Hints on Pronunciation

You will find all the words and phrases written both in French spelling and in a simplified spelling which you read like English. Don't use the French spelling, the one given in parentheses, unless you have studied French before. *Read the simplified spelling as though it were English.* When you see the French word for "where" spelled *oo*, give the *oo* the sound it has in the English words *too, boot,* etc. and not the sound it has in German or any other language you may happen to know.

Each letter or combination of letters is used for the sound it usually stands for in English and it *always* stands for that sound. Thus, *oo* is always pronounced as it is in *too, boo, boot, tooth, roost,* never as anything else. Say these words and then pronounce the vowel sound by itself. That is the sound you must use every time you see *oo* in the *Pronounciation* column. If you should use some other sound—for example, the sound of *oo* in *blood*—you might be misunderstood.

Syllables that are accented, that is, pronounced louder than others, are written in capital letters. In French, unaccented syllables are not skipped over quickly, as they are in English. The accent is generally on the last syllable in the phrase.

Hyphens are used to divide words into syllables to make them easier to pronounce. Curved lines (‿) are used to show sounds pronounced together without any break; for example, *day-z‿U H* meaning "some eggs," *kawm-B‿YANG* meaning "how much"'

Special Points

AY as in *may, say, play* but don't drawl it out as we do in English. Since it is not drawled it sounds almost like the *e* in *let*. Example: *ray-pay-TA Y* meaning "repeat."

J stands for a sound for which we have no single letter in English. It is the sound we have in *measure, leisure, usual, division, casualty, azure*. Example: *bawn-JOOR* meaning "Good day."

EW is used for a sound like *ee* in *bee* made with the lips rounded as though about to say the *oo* in *boot*. Example: *ek-skew-zay MWA* meaning "Excuse me."

U or UH as in *up, cut, rub, gun*. Examples: *nuf* meaning "nine," *juh* meaning "I."

U̱ or U̱H̱ as in *up, cut,* etc. but made with the lips rounded. Example: *D U̱H̱* meaning "two."

NG, N or M are used to show that certain vowels are pronounced through the nose, very much in the way we generally say *huh, uh-uh, uh-huh*. Examples: *lahnt-MAHNG* meaning "slowly," *juh kawm-PRAHNG* meaning "I understand," *NAWNG* meaning "no," *PANG* meaning "bread".

Memory Key

AY as in *day* but not so drawled.

U or UH as in *up*.

EW for the sound in *bee* said with the lips rounded.

J for the sound in *measure, division*.

NG, N or M for vowels pronounced through the nose.

GREETINGS AND GENERAL PHRASES

Hello or Good day—*bawn-JOOR (Bonjour)*

Good evening—*bawn-SWAR (Bonsoir)*

How are you?—*kaw-MAHN-T_ah-lay VOO? (Comment allez-vous?)*

Sir—*muss-'YUH (monsieur)*

Madam—*ma-DAHM (Madame)*

Miss—*mad-mwa-ZEL (Mademoiselle)*

Please—*SEEL voo PLAY (S'il vous plaît)*

Excuse me—*ek-skew-zay MWA (Excusez-moi)*

You're welcome—*eel nee ah pa duh KWA (Il n'y a pas de quoi)*

Yes—*WEE (Oui)*

No—*NAWNG (Non)*

Do you understand?—*KAWM-pruh-nay VOO? (Comprenez-vous?)*

I understand—*JUH kawm-PRAHNG (Je comprends)*

I dont understand—*juh nuh KAWM-prahng PA (Je ne comprends pas)*

Speak slowly, please—*par-lay LAHNT-mahng, seel voo PLAY (Parlez lentement; s'il vous plaît)*

Please repeat—*RAY-pay-tay, seel voo PLAY (Répétez s'il vous plaît)*

Location

When you need directions to get somewhere you use the phrase "where is" and then add the words you need.

Where is—*oo A Y (Où est)*
the restaurant—*luh RESS-to-RAHNG (le restaurant)*
Where is the restaurant?—*oo A Y luh RESS-to-RAHNG? (Où est le restaurant?)*
the hotel—*lo-TEL (l'hôtel)*
Where is the hotel?—*oo A Y lo-TEL? (Où est l'hôtel?)*

the railroad station—*la GAR (la gare)*
Where is the railroad station? —*oo A Y la GAR? (Où est la gare?)*
the toilet—*luh la-va-BO (le lavabo)*
Where is the toilet?—*oo A Y luh la-va-BO? (Où est le lavabo?)*

Directions

The answer to your question "Where is such and such?" may be "To the right" or "To the left" or "Straight ahead," so you need to know these phrases:

To the right—*ah DRWAT (à droite)*
To the left—*ah GOHSH (à gauche)*
Straight ahead—*too DRWA (tout droit)*

It is sometimes useful to say "Please show me."

Please show me—*seel voo PLAY, mawn-tray-MWA (S'il vous plaît, montrez-moi)*

If you are driving and ask the distance to another town it will be given you in kilometers, not miles.

Kilometer—*kee-lo-METR (kilomètre)*

One kilometer equals ⅝ of a mile.

For "twenty-one," "thirty-one" and so on, you say "twenty and one," "thirty and one," but for "twenty-two," "thirty-two" and so on, you just add the words for "two" and "three" after the words for "twenty" and "thirty," as we do in English.

Twenty-one—*van-t ay UNG* (*vingt-et-un*)

Twenty-two — *v a n t - D UH* (*vingt-deux*)

Thirty—*TRAHNT* (*trente*)

Forty—*KA - RAHNT* (*qua-rante*)

Fifty—*SAN-KAHNT* (*cin-quante*)

Sixty—*SWA-SAHNT* (*soix-ante*)

"Seventy," "eighty," "ninety" are said "sixty ten." "four twenties" and "four twenties ten."

Seventy—*swa - sahnt - DEESS* (*soixante-dix*)

Eighty—*k a t - r u h - V A N G* (*quatre-vingt*)

Ninety—*kat-ruh-van-DEESS* (*quatre-vingt-dix*)

One hundred—*SAHNG* (*cent*)

One thousand—*MEEL* (*mille*)

What's This?"

When you want to know the name of something you can say "What is it?" or "What's this?" and point to the thing you mean.

What is it?—*kess kuh SAY?* (*Qu'est-ce que c'est?*)

What's this?—*kess kuh suh-SEE?* (*Qu'est-ce que ceci?*)

What's that?—*Kess kuh say kuh SA?* (*qu'est-ce que c'est que ça?*)

Asking for Things

When you want something use the phrase "I want" and then add the name of the thing wanted. Always use "Please" —*seel voo PLAY.*

I want—*juh voo-DRAY (Je voudrais)*

some cigarettes—*day see-ga-RET (des cigarettes)*

I want some cigarettes—*juh voo-DRAY day see-ga-RET (Je voudrais des cigarettes)*

to eat—*mahn-JAY (manger)*

I want to eat—*juh voo-DRAY mahn-JAY (Je voudrais manger)*

. Here are the words for some of the things you may require. Each of them has the French word for "some" before it.

bread — *dew PANG (du pain)*

butter — *dew BUR (du beurre)*

soup—*duh la SOOP (de la soupe)*

meat—*duh la V⌣YAHND (de la viande)*

lamb—*dew moo-TAWNG (du mouton)*

veal—*dew VO (du veau)*

pork—*dew PAWR (du porc)*

beef—*dew BUF (du boeuf)*

eggs—*day-z⌣UH (des oeufs)*

vegetables—*day lay-GEWM (des légumes)*

salad—*duh la sa-LAD (de la salade)*

sugar—*dew SEWKR (du sucre)*

salt—*dew SEL (du sel)*

pepper—*dew PWAVR (du poivre)*

milk—*dew LAY (du lait)*

drinking water—*duh LO paw TA-bluh (de l'eau potable)*

a cup of tea—*ewn TASS duh TAY (une tasse de thé)*

a cup of coffee—*ewn TASS duh ka-FAY (une tasse de café)*

—————★—————

67

potatoes—*day PAWM duh TAYR* (*des pommes de terre*)

string beans—*day ah-ree-ko VAYR* (*des haricots verts*)

cabbage—*day SHOO* (*des choux*)

carrots—*day ka-RAWT* (*des carottes*)

peas—*day puh-tee PWA* (*des petits pois*)

a glass of beer—*ung VAYR duh B_YAYR* (*un verre de bière*)

a bottle of wine—*ewn boo-TAY_ee duh VANG* (*une bouteille de vin*)

some matches—*day-z_ah-lew-MET* (*des allumettes*)

the bill—*la-dees-YAWNG* (*l'addition*)

Money

To find out how much things cost, you say:

How much?—*kawm-B_YANG?* (*Combien?*)

The answer will be given in francs, sous, and centimes. Five centimes equal one sou, twenty sous or one hundred centimes equal one franc.

centime—*sahn-TEEM* (*centime*)

sou—*SOO* (*sou*)

franc—*FRAHNG* (*franc*)

Time

When you want to know what time it is you say really "What hour is it?"

What time is it?—*kel UR ay-t_EEL?* (*Quelle heure est-il?*)

For "One o'clock" you say "It is one hour."

One o'clock—*eel ay-t_EWN UR* (*Il est une heure*)

For "Two o'clock" you say, "It is two hours."

Two o'clock—*eel ay DUH-Z_UR* (*Il est deux heures*)

"Ten past two" is "Two hours ten."

Ten past two—*duh-z UR DEESS* (*deux heures dix*)
"Quarter past five" is "Five hours and quarter."
Quarter past five—*sank UR ay KAR* (*cinq heures et quart*)
"Half past six" is "Six hours and half."
Half past six—*see-z UR ay duh-MEE* (*six heures et demi*)
"Quarter of eight" is "Eight hours less the quarter."
Quarter of eight—*wee-t UR mwang luh KAR* (*huit heures moins le quart*)

When you want to know when a movie starts or when a train leaves, you say:

At what hour—*ah kel ur* (*à quelle heure*)
begins—*kaw-MAHNSS* (*commence*)
the movie—*luh see-nay-MA* (*le cinéma*)
When does the movie start? —*ah kel ur kaw-MAHNSS luh see-nay-MA?* (*A quelle heure commence le cinéma?*)

the train—*luh TRANG* (*le train*)
leaves—*PAR* (*part*)
When does the train leave?—*ah kel ur par luh TRANG?* (*A quelle heure part le train?*)
Yesterday—*ee-YAYR* (*hier*)
Today—*o-joord-WEE* (*aujourd'hui*)
Tomorrow—*duh-MANG* (*demain*)

The days of the week

Sunday—*dee-MAHNSH* (*dimanche*)
Monday—*LUN-DEE* (*lundi*)
Tuesday—*MAR-DEE* (*mardi*)
Wednesday—*MAYR-kruh-DEE* (*mercredi*)

Thursday—*JUH-DEE* (*jeudi*)
Friday—*VAHN-druh-DEE* (*vendredi*)
Saturday—*SAM-DEE* (*samedi*)

★———————★

Numbers

One—*UNG* (*un*)
Two—*DUH* (*deux*)
Three—*TRWA* (*trois*)
Four—*KATR* (*quatre*)
Five—*SANK* (*cinq*)
Six—*SEESS* (*six*)
Seven—*SET* (*sept*)
Eight—*WEET* (*huit*)
Nine—*NUF* (*neuf*)
Ten—*DEESS* (*dix*)
Eleven—*AWNZ* (*onze*)
Twelve—*DOOZ* (*douze*)

Thirteen—*TREZ* (*treize*)
Fourteen *KA-TAWRZ* (*quatorze*)
Fifteen—*KANZ* (*quinze*)
Sixteen—*SEZ* (*seize*)
Seventeen — *DEESS - SET* (*dix-sept*)
Eighteen — *DEEZ - WEET* (*dix-huit*)
Nineteen—*DEEZ-NUF* (*dix-neuf*)
Twenty—*VANG* (*vingt*)

Other Useful Phrases

The following phrases will be useful:

What is your name?—*kaw-MAHNG voo-z̲ ah-puh-lay VOO?* (*Comment vous appelez-vous?*)

My name is——*juh ma-PEL —* (*Je m'appelle—*)

How do you say *table* in French?—*kaw-MAHNG deet voo* table *ang frahn-SAY?* (*Comment dites-vous* table *en français?*)

I am an American — *juh SWEE - Z̲ ah - may - ree - KANG* (*Je suis Américain*)

I am your friend—*juh SWEE vawtr ah-MEE* (*Je suis votre ami*)

Please help me—*ay-day MWA seel voo PLAY* (*Aidez-moi s'il vous plaît*)

Where is the camp?—*oo ay luh KAHNG?* (*Où est le camp?*)

Take me there—*muh-nay-z̲ ee MWA* (*Menez-y moi*)

Good-by—*o ruh-VWAR* (*Au revoir*)

Additions and Notes

Thank you—*mayr-SEE (merci)*   I want—*juh VUH (je veux)*

The expression—*juh voo-DRAY*—is a polite way of saying "I want"; it really means "I would like." *juh VUH* is much stronger and should be used only when making a strong request or demand.

Additional Expressions

I am hungry — *jay FANG (J'ai faim)*

I am thirsty — *jay SWAF (J'ai soif)*

Stop!—*ALT! (Halte!)*

Come here!—*vuh-NAY-Z ee-SEE! (Venez ici!)*

Right away—*toot SWEET (Tout de suite)*

Come quickly!—*vuh-nay VEET! (Venez vite!)*

Go quickly!—*ah-lay VEET! (Allez vite!)*

Help!—*o suh-KOOR! (Au secours!)*

Bring help!—*ah-lay shayr-SHAY dew suh-KOOR! (Allez chercher du secours!)*

You will be rewarded—*voo suh-RAY ray-kawm-pahn-SAY (Vous serez récompensé)*

Where are the American soldiers?—*oo SAWNG lay sawl-DA-Z ah-may-ree-KANG? (Où sont les soldats américains?)*

Which way is north?—*duh-kel ko-TAY ay luh NAWR? (De quel côté est le nord?)*

Which is the road to—?—*kel ay luh shuh-MANG poor—? (Quel est le chemin pour—?)*

Draw me a map—*fet MWA ung kraw-KEE (Faites-moi un croquis)*

Take me to a doctor—*kawn-dwee-zay-MWA shay-z ung dawk-TUR (Conduisez-moi chez un docteur)*

Take cover!—*met-ay VOO-Z ah la-BREE! (Mettez-vous à l'abri!)*

★

71

Gas!—*gahz!* (*Gaz!*)

Danger!—*dahn-JAY!* (*Danger!*)

Watch out!—*pruh-nay GARD!* (*Prenez garde!*)

Be careful!—*fet ah-tahnss-YAWNG!* (*Faites attention!*)

Wait!—*ah-tahn-DAY!* (*Attendez!*)

Good luck—*bawn SHAHNSS* (*Bonne chance*)

France has been plundered by the Nazis to such an extent that the people are deprived of even the bare necessities of life. Don't make their plight more difficult by buying things that they so desperately need. It might cause great hardship and in the end bring about a condition that will make your own job a harder one. It is always a strain on our supply lines to feed people of liberated countries. Don't strain them further. And remember too, that the money you put aside today will be of far greater value to you when you return to civil life.